EVOLUTIONARY

POETRY
FOR THE SOUL
VOLUME III

BY
MADAME BUTTERFLI

PO Box 34093 St. Louis, MO 63134

www.madamebutterfli.com

Evolutionary: Poetry for the Soul Volume 3/ Madame Butterfli. – 1st ed.
Cover and Interior Design by Manika Felix
Author's photo by Excell Graham
ISBN-13: 978-1519173164
ISBN-10: 1519173164

Table of Contents

DEDICATION

First of all, I thank God for speaking to me and through me. There are times when I have no idea why I write what I do, but it is always revealed to me. For that, I couldn't be more appreciative.

I would also like to thank my children for being patient with me. There are times when all they want is mommy, but mommy is busy writing. I love you both!

Last, but not at all the least, I would like to thank my faithful readers and supporters. May God abundantly bless you in every area of life. I am forever grateful for you all.

THE MASTER'S BLUEPRINT

The mission that was deposited in my heart was designed exclusively for me

I was created with intent, no other will fit

My lines and angles, were perfectly patterned for the master's

blueprint

So look at me and know that in spite of what you think, I am who God created me to be

Strategically planted in time and place to walk purposefully in His plan

My destiny cannot be overtaken by man, it is in the master's hands

GROW

Of myself I freely give so that I may be
restored

Just as the transition of a
streaming river, constantly
renewed is the life of a giver

Stagnation breeds impurity, seek fluidity

An open hand is always
replenished, you reap what you sow

A liberal heart is never empty,
limitless love will flow

Seek to give just as you receive and
consistently

GROW

MIRACLES

Miracles happen right before our very eyes

Sometimes we see them, other times we don't

Our gratitude gives us hope,

never falling into a pit of despair

There is always a solution right there

Pray for a light when darkness creeps in,

an attempt to take your will to win

Victory is inevitable to those who realize the miracles right before their very eyes

It is impossible to be discouraged with
the evidence of glory in your life

You did not make it this far alone

Recognize the miracles that have pushed
you all along

SMILE

From a humbled heart, true love flows

Making the method honorable, in spite of the burden carried

All ills and issues buried

What is left rises above

compassion and love

The currency that translates into all languages and is felt through a smile

A smile that stretches farther than 1,000 words

A glow of affection that burns deep into one's

soul, making it easy to remember

Your tests can create bitterness, or

a lasting ember that will not be doused

The true sincerity of your smile

CHILDREN

Teach a child the right things and they will never depart

They are a reflection of what is in your heart

A filter that retains the good and the bad,

not holding back when they are angry or sad

Steer them in the right direction, correcting where you may have been misguided

They will magnify what they hear from the main source of their little ears

Be careful to give them your best in order to make it over the years

MOUNTAINS MOVE

Mountains are high, but they will move

We can go wherever we choose

Take the scenic route or the freeway

Whatever you do, do not stay in an unproductive state of mind

Put worry and frustration aside

Success and failure are in the words that you speak

Discouragement will bind your feet

Proceed with grace to your desired place

You can climb if you wish, but mountains will move

Only you can determine the amount of faith used

WINGS OF STEEL

My heart has wings of steel

It soars above all heaviness, not to be
weighed down by the winds of change
nor storms of opposition

My heart flies freely as if it were on the
path of least resistance

It rests on clouds, love is abound and the
resource of my force

I will not come down, but float at eagle's
altitude

Sometimes you win, sometimes you lose,
but my heart has wings of steel

My attitude is not determined by how I
feel

SOUND OF PEACE

The beauty of the sound of peace echoes
in my spirit,

overshadowing the protests against
pacification

Undefeated harmonies willfully drown the
flirtation of fear

Enduring the urge to conform to the
simple,

exploring the depths of that which is
unidentifiable yet felt within

There is only a matter of time

before what is inside will be

revealed with brightness just as a light

The reign of darkness will end, freeing
tormented

Souls suffering in silence

no longer violated

The beauty of the sound of peace will
echo for all to hear

Lingering in their spirits, breaking down
barriers that were created by defeat

REVOLVING AROUND YOU

All that I say and do revolves around you

When life seems so unfair and no one else
cares, you are the one who sees me
through

I often lie in bed thinking when I could be
out drinking, but my time with you is well
spent

Serenity overflows and swallows me up
whole, but that has not

always been the case

Your amazing grace covered me during
many times I could not see was ahead or
standing directly in front of me

I never have to call, you are right there
carrying me, lifting my arms and my
hands

When I could not stand you never let me
fall

I can truly say that for most of my days, you have been at the center of them all

I will continue to say what I need to say and do what I need to do in order to keep my life totally revolving around you

AGAINST THE TIDE

Boldness and revelation are your companions while going against the tide,

with an abundance of hope and a steady stride

Your destination may be far off, but your starting point is no longer visible

Returning is incomprehensible

You've come too far to throw in the towel

Do everything within your power except worry about how

As you progress, more revelation will come,

giving you the boldness to

continue forth

With an abundance of hope and a steady stride,

it will only become natural to go against the tide

OVERFLOWING

Such pleasure fills my mind

As I awake from my slumber and open my eyes, grateful for new blessings and a new day

All oppression has melted away

I look forward to letting the virtue from within arise

I am filled with content, there is no disguise

Every day is a surprise, with laughter and cheer

I'm so appreciative to have you near

I am never empty within, but overflowing with joy and filled to the brim

WARRIOR

No one notices a loser, you are a warrior within

If you constantly have to fight, it's because you're a champion

Don't become apprehensive,

exhausted, or quit

Your battles are not won by luck, but because you never give up

Keep the faith,

Never cease to contend and

overcome from day to day

If everyone left you alone, you never would've become strong

Don't curse your enemies, always bless They are the secret to your success

A SIGN

God, give me a sign

Put a thought in my mind

How do I know when it is time?

Will the clouds hover?

Will the leaves turn over?

Then again, the sun may beam just as a
spotlight on my dream

Will the phone ring, or should I just dial?

They say that there is no traffic along the
extra mile

Should I keep cramming or sign up for
the test?

The body gets wearier after

prolonged rest

How can I tell?

Will you give me a sign?

Present it so boldly that it will be recognized by the blind?

Do I continue to watch and interpret what I see, advancing haphazardly?

Will there be a plan to unfold?

My pages are long, yet I still do as I'm told

I'll let go of the questions, what's mine is mine

Everything comes in due time

AGAPE

There is a love that is so genuine, that it
ignores every fault

It forgives every mistake, whether or not
you reciprocate

An unconditional love that some never
feel, allows every wound of your heart to
heal

It cleanses every thought,

regulates your mind

Leaves every ill feeling behind

A love that surges through like an
electrical charge, releasing past negativity
and harm

It chills your soul, renewing and

replacing the old

You never have to search, it is
always there
available to replenish like a gust of fresh
air

GRATITUDE

As you count your blessings, more will
appear

You will go from a frown to
grinning ear to ear

We tend to overlook what seems to be
small,

which turns out to be the most
important of all

If we change our focus, we will be amazed
to see that our worst day may actually be
our best

Due to the beneficial lessons from our
tests, our source of gratitude abundantly
grows

It will seem frivolous to complain,

when we realize that from our gratitude
we emotionally, mentally, and spiritually
gain

STEADILY BUILT

Build me steadily, don't forget any stones,

so that I will be able to stand on my own

Put me on a solid foundation, so that I
resist temptation

Take extra care not to leave out any
screws,

so that I will be able recognize all of your
cues

Make faithfulness and stillness my anchor
so that I will not be moved

Every good and perfect gift comes from
you

Seal every crack and crevice with
your approval

Your presence will not leave and
no other will get in

I will be continuously filled and will not
have to pretend

Cover me with your wings of

protection,

So that I will consistently go in the right
direction

What you build will not be shaken or
moved,

but will stand steadily, leaving the enemy
confused

BE YOURSELF

To live according to one's own convictions
is to truly live

Free from the opinions that others give

You can look in the mirror every day and
say, "I do what it takes to make this world
a better place."

From you others grow

Your actions are not for show, but
represent what is within

You can't help but to win

No one can discredit the truth

Stop living for everyone else and just be
you

KEEP A LIGHT ON

Take the time to liberate your mind from
all of the negative judgments of yourself

You are what you say you are,

you have the right to choose life or death

We are all a product of our thoughts,

choose the good over the bad

What we think, we will most

definitely speak

So, keep a light on within

It's up to you to decide how happy you
will be

Whether the sun shines or

darkness looms is completely up to you

TURN-AROUND

Consider the respectable, don't pervert a
good thing

To what dwells in your conscience, your
dialogue will always lean

Take inventory any time of the year and
spring clean

You will move in the direction of your
thoughts, concentrate on the right things

A blissful life is produced by a blissful
mind

Leave all of the junk behind

Decide today to have a positive flow

Your situation will turn around

before you know

FOUNTAIN

Give me a fountain where I can drink and
never thirst

Pour out your love, fill my soul

until it bursts-

abounding with jubilation that fills the air,

sharing it with those who surround me
would only be fair

We all seek the joy that you bring

Many desire for the weight of their loads
to melt

Who can keep a fountain to

themselves?

I will sing and speak of your love
relentlessly,

releasing it as a dove, for all to be free

UNIQUE

Just as the print of our hands, we are all unique

from the way that we think, to the way that we speak

The most difficult thing may be to retain who you are, while being bombarded with what "looks like a star"

Know that there is value in your true self

From the abundance of your heart, there is much wealth

Believe that you were created with a purpose that was custom built

In no other socket you will fit

Acceptance of yourself all that you need

Others will catch up when you take the lead

GLOW

When you wake up with joy, don't let
another bring you down

Your entire night was spent

replacing a frown

Come up to my level of peace, or we can't
speak right now

If you refuse to surrender to

negativity, it will bow

Take your peace with you wherever you
go

without saying a word, it will show

Let it glow, lifting every spirit that is low

MEDICATED DART

Love finds a way in,
seeping through our thick skin
Permeating our bleeding heart
Cupid has a medicated dart
Mind spins, lips grin
There's no going back once you're all in
No one regrets the feeling once it's gone
We just carry on
Waiting for our next turn
Hoping that it doesn't burn

CONFLICT EDUCATION

Our conflicts are an education, we can
each learn from our own

Life is too short to circle the same zone

Move forward and educate who you can

Be supportive, but not entangled,
you must be free to loose the bound

Lemons can't change your
sweetness, so let the sour drown

Decline the distractions of those who
poke holes into your soul,

blocking those who need you most

Purpose thieves, hijacking not only your
dreams, but those who are willing to
listen, to learn,

AND to go higher

Never cease to inspire

PASSION

It is said that actions speak louder than words

If so, nouns are no greater than verbs

A person doing is more fulfilled than a person being

Hearing is trumped by seeing

A victorious life is full of meaning, bringing life to a vision, constantly on a mission

Resting to refresh, that is all

Pursuing passion until the closing call

WHISPERED PRAYER

The skies above are not high enough to
measure my gratitude

Nothing deserved, but by your grace

When you call, I answer with haste

You have done so many marvelous things,

looking past all of my faults and seeing
my needs

Never fear, God is always there,

answering the most quietly

whispered prayer

UNCHAIN

Unchain me from my post, so that I may run free

Unguarded and unrestrained,

let peace run through my brain and throughout the streets of

tyranny and persecution

freeing every slave

Newness will constantly pour into the air that we breathe

lifting those who are suffocating on their knees

Give independence in thoughts and deeds enabling them to see with transparency,

that they, are in fact, equipped with all that they need

INSIDE

What is inside, will inevitably show

There's a lot more to ourselves that we
actually know

The current day reveals more that the one
before, continuing to make its way down
to our core

We can't know what we love without
knowing who we are

You are not all of the labels and
stereotypes that others have placed

Let go of what "they" say

Do not allow your presence be a waste

Make a difference wherever you go

It may seem small, but you know,

that good seeds planted will grow-

blossoming into the most beautiful things
reminding us to let our heart take the
lead

Life may not be a walk in the park, it is what you make it

If you appreciate the things around you, you'd be surprised at what you might get

It's not quantity that makes abundance, but quality
Good things are not always free

Living life with a tainted perception will affect what you see

Change your mind and change your world

Read between the lines and look for what is not there

Dare to dream, open your eyes and live

Believe that getting what you want is fair

UNDEFEATED

Be unapologetic for the grace on your life,
unwilling to step back and dim your light

Even though you may be uncertain about
the future that lies ahead, be unrelenting
about what has already been said

The joy deep inside of you is unfeigned,
unfounded due to the circumstances

Not easily understood to most

However, it's not unreachable unless you
underestimate the importance of
underlying values

that make you unbreakable in

unacceptable conditions

Realize that you are never

unguarded and don't become

unfurled

Remain unceasing and unshakable in this uncivil world

TIME AND PLACE

Trust that the crooked path will be made straight

Keep walking in the direction of your fate

No matter how long you have stalled, its never too late

Good things do come to those who wait

Leave room for patience to be your mate

Time stands still for no one, it's easy to operate in haste

Stay grounded with perseverance until you find that special place

Permanent or temporal, believe that nothing is a waste

ART OF NATURE

Breathtaking is the art of nature,

smoothly, it comes together

Many colors coordinating perfectly
regardless of the weather

If our lives were as the art of nature, what
would we be?

An ideal spring day, or the worst blizzard
that one could dream?

Will the birds sing or fly south?

Would the grass die or sprout?

Our wind, hot and stifling or cool and
gentle?

Will your presence be carefree, or cause
for layers of covering?

Summer, Autumn, Winter, or Spring

As breathtaking as the art of nature I will

be

Allowing all things to come together
simply

DO RIGHT

Frivolity will pass

The underhanded may seem to get ahead fast

Only that which is honest will last

Build what you have on sound principles,
or you may just watch it wither away like
grass

Right before your very eyes

There's no honor in lies

The taller the building, the bigger the fall

It's your call

We answer to our every deed, it's best not
to be driven by greed

An honest heart breeds the best results,

wonderful blessings, not to be confused
with luck

GIVE AND LIVE

We are not created to stand alone

Our abilities are to share with people
everywhere

There is a newness of mind that comes
with giving,

a refreshing of the spirit

Regeneration occurs when you share a
piece of yourself with the world

You may be answering a cry or giving
insight to someone who thought they
might die

You never know who you may affect,
don't hold back

As you serve others, you bless yourself

A sound mind is the greatest wealth

SEARCH FOR THE LOST

The knowledge of good is written in our hearts

When we ignore what is within, we ignore who we are

It may not be easy the first time around, but before you know it, your true self is nowhere to be found

The search for the lost is a journey alone

To what you have within, always hold on

Trusting what you know may be a lonely road,

but at the end you will know that

those who detoured are further behind,

the search for the lost takes a lot of time

Some find it, others don't

Stick with your heart, never gamble

Even a little bit of right is ample to stand against a world of wrong

In that case, you realize that you are never alone

JUDGE YOUR HEART

We all have our own faults and thorns,
which keep us searching all the more

A quiet urge that won't allow us to settle
for less than our best,

makes it easy to maneuver any difficult
mess

Don't let your standards falter, keep them
high

They control how you react in any
situation that may arise

Seek to do no harm and keep your hands
clean

Our intentions always guide our deeds

DIFFERENT

When we call on God, he doesn't look at
our skin,

but answers our prayers based on what is
within

What if we as people were the same and
stopped abusing others in religion's
name?

Having the heart of God is not going by
what we see, or from our limited
knowledge of what things appear to be

It's reaching out for an understanding of
more,

following an unction beyond our
boundaries to explore

There is nothing new under the sun,

yet no two

people are the same

By accepting our differences, we can only gain

TIME

You are all that I need,

when my heart is so heavy that it wants to bleed

If I follow you, there will be no mistakes

You make it clear what path to take

In spite of the circles that appear to be my fate,

what is twisted will become straight

Calm my spirit as I wait

Whenever you get here, it won't be too late

BLIND

We have homeless with homes

Penniless with an income

Those who are lonely with friends

Orphans with families

Spinsters with spouses

Famished people with plenty of food,

thirsty standing next to a fountain

Unclean standing in a shower

Weak people with a whole lot of power

Living decades on borrowed time

Unorganized, yet everything is in line

We look, but don't see

Speak, but say nothing

Move ahead, but never pass

Continuing to mask,

dormancy with busy work

Only fooling ourselves

Time always tells

CHOICES

What a difference a little time can make, with the people that you meet along the way

Some good, some not

A few are friends, others plot

Be who you are, but careful walking in

Figure out who wants attention and who is a true friend

You'd be surprised that it may not be as it seems

The best one may be who you never see

Choosing wisely makes your world a better place

One wrong move may bring a disgrace

MIND RIGHT

Alone time is the best

Some circumstances we don't recognize
as stress

We incorporate things into our day to day
that will gradually eat our lives away

Don't be afraid to be alone to form
thoughts and opinions on your own

Pessimism cannot purge if it is
continuously fed

Some parts of our being are better off
dead

It's a necessity to get your mind right,

a process that requires patience, nothing
happens over night

The more stability that you have, the
easier it is to fight

for the peace that we all deserve inside

Let go and let freedom ride

BE BETTER

Our experiences affect our opinions and
mold who we become

In order to be a better person, you must
face the worst

How else will you be able to compare?

Enduring harsh treatment will make you
responsible for showing that you care

Consider it a challenge to rise above

Combat hatred with the peace of a dove

Some will never know it until you show it

It is possible to create what you never see

Be unaccommodating, that's the key

A non-conformist to oppressive things

Standing for what is right may send you

up a creek without a paddle

the best part about it, is that it's not your battle

THE WALL

There is a wall that is too high to climb

Is there a door or a window?

Perhaps, it's not meant to enter

If I break it down, I may get bit

If I scale it, the ground I may hit

No one waits next to a stone wall

There may be hesitation if the end of the sun beam is on the other side

There is only so long that you can mark time

hoping that when the day breaks, it will lead you in a

different direction

A place just as pleasant and free

The curiosity about the wall may still never leave

CLEARLY

What seems clear, is not

Find what is hidden beneath

Look for what you don't see

Pray as you search deeply, uncovering a
multitude of thoughts one by one

obtaining forgiveness for our faults

Converting to like images and unique
beings,

Who surrender to our purpose without
fleeing

Finding the definition of radiance while
displaying

The clouds break

There is no longer any mistake

WISDOM'S FRIEND

As wisdom takes the lead, I will follow

If it speaks to my heart, I will listen

If it stops, I will also

No good thing happens independently, wisdom is the ally

It is not the where and the how that is important, it's why

Authenticity produces such and the counterfeit causes waste

Purity always has the finest taste

Think before you leap and you can bear anything that you face

Wisdom also has a friend named grace, who comes along when least expected just as your faith is being tested

Stick with them and you can't go wrong

It's not about the swift, but the strong

CHANGE

The perfect will of God is a delightful place to be

It is a place of strength that carries you when you can't see

Burdens are lifted from a heavy heart

All that is required is to do your part

It is impossible to remain the same from day to day

When you learn from every experience, the only choice that you have is to change

It's to your own benefit not to get stuck in old ways

Time never stops, it will leave you in a cave

Although your values may not change, you can still become as current as the day

DAILY EFFORT

A smile from within is rarely contained

Daily effort is not in vain

When persistence is not disturbed,
progress occurs

Never hesitate to fight for what is right,

the reward is transcendental

Adjust your mind to fall in line with what
is pleasing to your soul

Only then, will happiness unfold

THE ANSWER

There is a way, even if none is perceived

An answer to all unanticipated needs

may not be close, but it's never out of reach

Think higher than what you observe,

Know that your prayers are heard and the answer surpasses your own resolution

Keep going, resistance is a sign that you are moving,

building your muscle as you progress

It's all part of the test

The strong survive and the weak fall off

Very few are willing to pay the cost

BY INTENT

Anytime is too soon to give up

Nothing happens by luck

Doing what you are supposed to do and being where you are supposed to be is the key

Any achievement is by intent

Be watchful of how your time is spent

We all have the same twenty-four hours

Be frivolous or discerning

Waste time complaining, or start learning

Decide not to give in

Quitters never win

ON TIME

The bus will only come once, it doesn't
circle back around

Maybe you can catch one on the other
side of town

The driver may have seen you, but had to
depart

You can't hold everyone else up because
one is straggling behind

From now on, leave early and be the first
in line

Waiting longer will save you a lot of time

Everything else seems important until you
miss your goal

If you focus on what is in front of you,
your life will never be on hold

ALANO

Such a splendid creation of life

Handsome, talented, creative, and bright

I would say that the sky is the limit to
what you can do,

but don't forget that there are footprints
on the moon

You are loved more than you will ever
know

I take pleasure in watching you grow,

physically, mentally, spiritually, and in
every other way

I'm grateful to have you brighten my day

Always remember that you are one of a
kind

Be true to yourself and you will never fail
to win,

All of the power that you need lies within

BLESSED

Count your blessings no matter what the
state

Lack of gratitude is the worst bait

You may not be where you want, but have
all that you need

Appreciation leads to greater things

Keeping your mind from the pit is vital

Nothing is final

Your resilience will inspire

Many succumb through the fire

Shine all of the way through

never overtaken, inner strength can't be
shaken

Know that what is on the other side is
exceptional,

and that favor is perpetual

UNDER HIS WINGS

He loves us whether we return it
or not
More than we love ourselves
Throughout all of your difficulties, you
learn
His grace is a gift that cannot be earned,
but is given
Just because you are and He is
Under His wings of healing, we live
We trample our enemies under our heels,
as we walk forward, never looking behind
having faith that all will fall in line
Step by step, one day at a time
Know that the ending is written
Our task is to believe with thanksgiving

THE TREE

The storm may rage, but my soul is still

I will not be moved by incapacity, nor will
I flee from vexation

My roots, only plucked by the planter

The wind causes my seeds to scatter

The sun still shines and the clouds never
stay, nor are they visible without the rays

Allow nothing to distract your gaze

There is more depth to what you perceive

Focus on your faith and know what not to
believe

Your advocate never leaves

FREEDOM

There is so much power in the freedom of the mind

Contentment in leaving all apprehension behind

Our thoughts change nothing, only actions and deeds

Patience and timing will allow us to succeed,

if you don't trust them, your fears you will constantly feed

Those who find their own freedom can seek the same for others

Without it, you will have the urge to control your brother

Never discerning that our differences are our strengths

As they all work together, we bear an impeccable gift

DARE TO DREAM

Be bold, stand strong, dare to dream

It won't always be as easy as it looks or as difficult as it seems

To reach your maximum potential, you can't cave in

Those who take the easy way out, never really win

You may slip, trip, or fall, but persistence is the solution

You can't let past failures become a pollution

Dreams only die with our permission

If you come up short, don't lose sight of your vision

CLIPPED WINGS

Birds with clipped wings can only fly so far

Their surroundings mold them into who they are

Birds with clipped wings can only fly so high

Never reaching their full potential, not knowing why

Plateauing or falling, living a life with no true calling

Rarely escaping oppression, constantly fighting depression

In order to grow, you must leave the habitat of those who clip your wings

You may be devoured, or starve, or wind up in the way of harm

The fortunate find grace, allowing them to be in a safe place

until their wings begin to grow, full,
healthy, and ready for flight

Remembering where they once were, they
are not afraid to become fully fledged,
nor are they afraid of heights

PROPELLING

Lies infect, honesty brings lasting respect

It takes integrity to deal fairly, not
sanctioning yourself to shame

Act as if someone is always watching, it
will drive your enemies insane

Feed your mind or it will devour itself

Intelligence is true wealth

Problems are lessons in disguise

Learn, apply, and thrive

Don't be afraid to transform, grow, and
move on

Propelling to achieve wonderful things

Not allowing anyone to clip your wings

THE WALK

Guiding others to the light and not to the dark

is what sets good leaders apart

Knowing how to steadily gaze into the distance, while not ignoring the now

By the who, when, and what, we discover the how

You can't give directions to a place where you have never been

Your experiences help others to win

Let go of anxiety and persevere until the end

Those who fall short, get up again and again

All that matters is that you never give up

Success is not merely good luck

SURVIVAL

Our quest for knowledge is as long as our lives

Having wisdom along with understanding it's the only way to survive

Our own feelings, we must put aside

No one has all of the answers, collectively we fight

Our strength is when we unite

If we lose sight of our mission, we fail

Allowing injustice and inequality to prevail

ANSWER TO MY CALL

I don't lose a thing by giving my all

When I cry out, there is an answer to my
call

When I am out on a limb and feel alone,
is when I realize that God takes care of his
own

That is why I continue to pray and call on
his name

I know that my answer is never far away

OVERCOME

A snowflake is minute compared to a blizzard,

just as a raindrop to a hurricane

Focus on the minute and be overtaken by the great

Never lose faith

Overcome small battles to win the war,

not being preoccupied with keeping score

Gallantly fight

Enduring the night until the day breaks,

unrepressed by mistakes

Standing on every stone that has been thrown

Only look back in order to see how you've grown and become unaffected by the minute

Ignore lies and seek truth

HEAR, SEE, BE

Grateful that I can hear, see, and be

All that I need

In the right place at the right time

Pursuing the betterment of mankind

Love is blind and covers a multitude of faults

From our own experiences, we are taught

If we choose to take heed

Graciously proceed or stand still

Be broken or healed

Bitter or sweet

Confident or compete

All things in humility and not vanity for the sake of your own sanity

Hear, see, and be

Shackles are temporary, you are forever free

FOLLOW YOUR HEART

Follow your heart and your dreams

Live on purpose, work hard behind the scenes

Believe that good things happen in due time, tears come to an end

The most difficult battles have the greatest wins

Pain has an expiration date

You level of perseverance determines your fate

No task is to small for your undivided attention

Don't forget to search for intentions

The worst will ruin the best

Follow your heart and your dreams

Stand firm in your convictions

They are not meant for restriction,
but to allow you to remain free from
insane addictions,
bonds that are difficult to break
Remain in an untainted place

THOSE WORDS

Do you love me? I want to know

Many have said it, but their actions didn't show

Tell me something different, but yet the same

How do you feel when you hear my name?

Do you smile without thinking? Does your heart leap?

Do you think about me at night before you go to sleep?

Whisper something and send a tingle down my spine

Tell me that you will always be mine

Before you push me over into the deep
end, knowing that I can't even swim

Without saying those words, let me

know

That you have no intention of letting me

go

FREEDOM AND LIGHT

One may not be behind bars, but there
are several types of jail

Minds and spirits in captivity, many
unaware

Our thoughts have the ability to lead us
into a cave

Off of our path of destiny we become
darkness's slave

The lamp in our minds slowly fade

Life becomes dim, causing you to lose
your way

It's never too late to turn around,

freedom and light will soon be found

SUN

The sun surrounds and follows me all day

It seems as if I can't get away from it's rays

I've found all of the benefits that they give

Some are pertinent in order to live,

making it difficult to complain

Gratitude comes into play,

for the sun that shines night and day

SAME

My Father drives, I enjoy the scene

I depend on him for everything

He's there though turbulent times and peace

When I need him the most and when I feel that I need him the least

If I jump out of the car, he'll let me back in

A special type of friend

When I ask for forgiveness, he gives

He never changes, always the same

His love for me still remains

WORD SAYINGS

Let your words be few and wise, you will appear to be more intelligent in man's eyes

A soft answer turns away a storm, which may come in many ways, shapes, and forms

Choose your words carefully, season them with integrity

Words can be a friend or foe, only speak what you know

What you say in private will be repeated to many, avoid offending

It's impossible to evade every dart

Most importantly, speak your truth directly from your heart

MY PRAYER

Intensify my sight so that I may see the
mission as you do

All that you say is true and nothing
returns void

Every obstruction destroyed and cast far
away

My heart is nonjudgmental and will not
stray

I know that you have prepared what is
best for me this day

The reason why I trust no matter what my
enemies say

Hold us in the palm of your hand,
protecting us from hurt and harm

We have no cause for alarm

Every challenge faced: overcome

Free our hearts and allow us to love

By giving, we receive

more than we can conceive

Our rewards may not be seen, but are
more valuable than gold

Our stories to be told

BECAUSE

Just because I laugh, doesn't mean that I don't know sorrow

Just because I smile, doesn't mean that I've never cried

I sing because once I could only moan

I love because I experience hate

I am confident because I have feared

I overlook because I was once consumed

I am carefree because I was once burdened

I pray because I was once silenced

CLOUDS

I keep my thoughts high,

meditating through the clouds and the
haze

whether it's for minutes or days,

lose focus, regain

I surrender my mind.

So I know that my aspirations come from
you

My difficulties are a recipe for strength,

nourishment for my mind, body, and spirit

My obstacles are my exercise,

my conditioning for endurance

blessed assurance that when the clouds
pass the

sun beams

A reminder that things are not all of the

time what they seem

What you see is a product of my past

and

a preface to my future

SUPER

Explore and discover
Find what is hidden and uncover
Search for the lost
Listen to what isn't told
Do the impossible
Create the nonexistent
Think the unimaginable
Reach the unattainable
Live the illusion

SWEET HEARTS

Pain can turn a heart sour and become
defeat

Convert disappointments into a sweet
and tasty treat

Preserve your heart with diligence

Clean hearts maintain privilege

Contrary to popular belief,

setting rules for your heart will make you
free

TRANSFORM

The worst thing that ever happened can
become the best,

differentiating good and separating the
strong from the rest

My goals and the bigger picture will
always get me through

Keep moving and looking forward instead
of constantly checking the rear-view

the stubborn digress, evolving is always
part of progress

Through the worst situations, we become
our best

our willingness to transform is our major
test

THANKFUL FOR

What do I have to be thankful for?

All that is tangible and more

The new gifts that arrive each day and the
ones that never go away

What is now and is to come,

battles being fought that are already
won-

without violence or a gun

The consistent fire that burns inside

becoming more difficult to hide

My attitude of gratitude developed
during trying times

What do I have to be thankful for?

All of the above, but most of all,

the peace of a dove

IDOL

We've created a God who is nonexistent,

who has no regard for the well-being of divine creation of life

We've created a God who is deaf and dumb

Therefore, we rescue ourselves from our own fears and adversities

This God has no arms or helping hands and is unable to heal the land

God is love, but we've created one without,

leaving us burdened and in constant doubt

HARMONY

Appreciate each day and acknowledge it
for what it is,

a blessing and another chance to give

Our lives orchestrated in perfect harmony

Balanced to give each other the support
that we

need

Everything has a purpose if you look
around and see

From the grass, to the trees, and the little
squirrels that run free,

to the person that handed you a tissue
when you sneezed

All working together as a well-oiled
machine

Each one of us can live according to our dreams

creating a unique masterpiece

CHANGE

Change is imminent, unavoidable, a necessity

Resisted by the powers that be in an ever-changing society

May our values catch up with our technology

Let the younger generation lead our transformation into one nation

God and country is what they say as they kill innocent children in his name,

undermining the intelligence of our people and the integrity of the laws

Fatal character flaws

Land of the free governed by brutality

Change is imminent, unavoidable, a necessity

in order to continue on to a path of prosperity

and justice for all

Respond to the call

BEAUTIFULLY STRONG

When you look around and there is
nothing left,

only the lessons and memories that
you've kept

Be thankful and know that there is more

Just seek, and what was lost will be
restored

In a matter of time, the seeds that you
have planted will break though

and

what you have been cultivating all along

will finally appear

beautifully strong

LEFT AND RIGHT

I look to the left and to the right, there is
no one but you

All of my faith goes to the one who
demonstrates his perfect love

granting his favor, daily

Though storms arise, I refuse to complain

He has never abandoned, but always
protected,

replacing those who are no longer by my
side

with his angels to my left and right

RECONSTRUCTED

Our creator sees all, knows all, and has
our best interest at heart

When it seems as though your life is
falling apart,

you come to realize that you are being
reconstructed

A skylight is added with new windows and
doors

Shiny new things replace what was rotten
before

A new sound system so that you can hear
even more

We have to let go and trust with our
whole heart

Don't waste too much time stumbling in
the dark

A THANKFUL HEART

A thankful heart goes a long way

It makes all of the difference in what you
think and say,

changing the perspective of what you see
from day to day

It determines if you will learn or complain,
grow or remain the same

A thankful heart finds the positive and it
increases the more

An ingrate eats away at his own soul,

finding nothing but the worst, making her
own life a curse

Find something great or small to be
thankful for

Things may not be what you intended for

them to be,

but somewhere there is a blessing, if you
will only believe

REVELATION

I have no choice but acknowledge my humanity

My existence flows naturally, unrelentingly, overpowering, and unapologetically

My energy is reserved for being all that I was created to be, in spite of what surrounds me

I have no time left to consider the limitations and labels that have been given by those who aren't driven to surpass their own

Positive or negative, good or bad, truth is told

What is concealed shall be revealed and widely known

EXCELLENCE

Our excellence is determined by our
service to God,

we are his arms and legs

Open your ears to hear what he has said

From the substantial to the minute,

we choose to become as such

by our willingness to allow our hearts to
be touched

There is no secret to achieving excellence,

only move as directed

RELINQUISH

When I relinquish control, I am led to a
place that is picture perfect

Beyond famine, poverty, and disease

farther than the eyes can see

When I relinquish control, my spirit has
wings

that fly and take away unclean things

True power is in having none at all,

but being an instrument to the one who
orchestrates it all

PRAISES, I GIVE

New day rises, I am grateful for what it
brings
Bountiful blessings, my joy bells ring
Praises, I give to the creator of all things
Lord of lords and King of kings
You speak life where none exists
You carry those who have no strength
Amongst everything, you have a plan
One that is already written and in your
hands
So, I'll continue to go your way, with you
by my side
Tragedies do not cause me to hide
Knowing that they push me to my best,
full of power withstanding the tests
I will give all praises to the King of kings,
Creator of all, Lord of everything

LOVE YOUR NEIGHBOR

The love that you have placed inside of me is not only for me and mine,

but to love others with a heart that is blind

I am to treat my neighbors as myself

How can I love God and hurt everyone else?

It is not possible, he would call me a liar

So, I keep a mind full of patience instead of envious fire

A healthy life is full of love

Take advantage of the gift from God above

Override past hurt, torment, and pain

There is nothing to lose, only to gain

The love that God has place inside of me

is not only for me and mine

He has given it to me for the betterment of mankind

BEGIN NEW

Vow to begin new each day

Cast previous worries away

What you feel inside will always come out

Erase all doubt and calm your fears

All of the answers that you are searching
for are near

VISIONARY

I will close my eyes to see in the distance,

my nearsightedness does not affect my vision

Your goodness dictates my decision, not my limited point of view

The fullness of the world belongs to God to do whatever he may choose

I pray for his blessings and receive them as promised

I can't help but to be honest when I say that you are the only true way

Anything else is a delusion, a precursor to confusion

My own worries are put aside, I permit your thoughts to become mine

Any crisis is only a perception of time

ABOUT THE AUTHOR

MADAME BUTTERFLI

I am a mother, a minister, a poet, and a lover of life. I write daily about my journey to self-awareness and improvement. I believe that all change starts from within. We have to recognize where we excel and where we fall short in order to offer the world the best version of ourselves.

Made in the USA
Charleston, SC
27 October 2016